VALENTINE'S DAY

Written by Alice K. Flanagan

Illustrated by Shelley Dieterichs

Content Adviser: Professor Sherry L. Field, Department of Social Science Education, College of Education, The University of Georgia

Reading Adviser: Dr. Linda D. Labbo, Department of Reading Education, College of Education, The University of Georgia

C O M P A S S   P O I N T   B O O K S

MINNEAPOLIS, MINNESOTA

Compass Point Books
3722 West 50th Street, #115
Minneapolis, MN 55410

Visit Compass Point Books on the Internet at *www.compasspointbooks.com*
or e-mail your request to *custserv@compasspointbooks.com*

Editors: E. Russell Primm and Emily J. Dolbear
Designer: The Design Lab

Library of Congress Cataloging-in-Publication Data

Flanagan, Alice K.
  Valentine's day / Written by Alice K. Flanagan ; illustrated by Shelley Dieterichs.
    p. cm. — (Holidays and festivals)
  Includes bibliographical references and index.
  ISBN 0-7565-0088-5 (hardcover : lib. bdg.)
    1. Valentine's Day—Juvenile literature. [1. Valentine's Day. 2. Holidays.]
I. Dieterichs, Shelley, ill. II. Title. III. Series.
  GT4925 .F53 2002
  394.2618—dc21   2001001508

Table of Contents

How Valentine's Day Began 5

How Valentine's Day Got Its Name 6

Flowers for Valentine 9

How Valentine's Day Spread 12

The First Paper Valentines 17

Valentine's Day Comes to America 21

American Valentines 22

Things You Might See on Valentine's Day 24

What You Can Do on Valentine's Day 29

Glossary 30

Where You Can Learn More about Valentine's Day 31

Index 32

Roses are red. Violets are blue. I'm your friend. Are you mine, too?

These are words you might read on a **valentine**. Valentine's Day is an American holiday. It is **celebrated** on February 14.

On Valentine's Day, we give cards and small gifts to special people in our lives. We call the cards and gifts "valentines." Do you know why?

How Valentine's Day Began

Many stories tell how Valentine's Day began. Some people believe the holiday came from a **festival** that Romans celebrated more than 2,000 years ago. They called the festival *Lupercalia*. It was given in honor of the Roman god Lupercus.

Roman **shepherds** believed that Lupercus protected their crops and animals from hungry wolves. To thank Lupercus, the shepherds held a feast in his honor on February 15.

At that time, the Roman calendar was different from the one we use today. The month of February came later in the year. So on the feast of Lupercalia, the Romans also celebrated the beginning of spring.

The day before Lupercalia, all the girls put their names in a jar. Each boy drew a name. The girl whose name he chose became his partner for games. Sometimes, the two promised to marry each other.

How Valentine's Day
Got Its Name

The festival of Lupercalia changed when the Romans became **Christians**. The Romans did not believe in Lupercus any longer. They wanted to keep the holiday, however.

The Romans decided to rename the holiday Saint Valentine's Day. It was in honor of a Christian priest named Valentine. Valentine lived in Rome many years ago. There are many stories about this man.

In one story, Valentine broke the law. The **emperor** would not let any of his soldiers marry. He believed that single men made better soldiers. Valentine did not agree. He helped young men and women get married. The emperor put Valentine in prison for disobeying the law. Then, on February 14, A.D. 269, he put Valentine to death.

Christians never forgot Valentine's courage. Every year, on February 14, they honored him. They thought about what he did for love.

Later, the Christian Church said that Valentine was a saint. A saint is a holy person who helps others. Christians called Valentine the **patron saint** of people in love.

Flowers for Valentine

Another story tells how Valentine helped a blind girl to see. Valentine loved children. He also loved flowers and had a beautiful garden. Often he gave children flowers from his garden.

One day, the emperor put Valentine in prison because he would not pray to the Roman gods. Children brought flowers to Valentine in prison. They tossed them through the bars of the prison window. On the flowers, they put love notes to him. They drew birds and flowers on the notes.

Valentine made friends with a prison guard. The prison guard's daughter was blind. Valentine prayed that the girl might see. God answered Valentine's prayers and the girl's sight returned.

The emperor said he would free Valentine if he prayed to the

Roman gods. Valentine was a Christian and refused. The emperor put Valentine to death on February 14.

Before Valentine died, he wrote a note to the guard's daughter. He signed it "From your Valentine."

How Valentine's Day Spread

Over time, many Romans became Christians. Some moved to other countries and brought their holidays with them.

In time, people in England also celebrated Valentine's Day. They added some of their own **customs**.

In one custom, girls wrote boys' names on pieces of paper. They rolled the pieces of paper into a ball of clay. Then they dropped it into a bucket of water. Soon the clay ball fell apart. It was said that the girl would one day marry the boy whose name floated to the top.

Later, Valentine's Day spread to other countries. In Italy, young men and women met in flower gardens on Valentine's Day. They listened to music and read poems.

In Austria, Hungary, and Germany, Valentine's Day was a religious

feast day for boys. Each boy picked the name of a saint. He tried to live like that saint during the year.

In France, young men and women went to fancy dances on Valentine's Day. At the dance, the men gave the women flowers.

In Germany, girls believed they could find out who their husbands would be. On Valentine's Day, they planted onions in pots. Next to each onion, they placed the name of a boy. They put the pots near a fireplace. Then they waited for the first onion to grow. The girls believed that they would marry the boy whose name was nearest this onion.

The First Paper Valentines

Over the years, more and more people learned how to read and write. They sent love letters to their **sweethearts**. Later, these letters were called **valentines**.

People decorated valentines with hearts and flowers. They also drew birds and little babies on them.

Today, the oldest paper valentine is in the British Museum in London, England. The Duke of Orleans wrote that valentine to his wife in 1415. He was a prisoner in the Tower of London.

The English liked paper valentines very much. They wrote poems and then decorated them with ribbons and lace. Those who did not know what to write looked in a little book of poems called a valentine writer. A valentine writer cost a penny.

Most valentines at this time were made by hand. Sometimes, people asked artists to make valentines for them. Artists made fancy paper-lace valentines.

It cost a lot to send a letter by mail. Most people gave their hand-made valentines to their **sweethearts** themselves.

Later, the cost of mailing a letter dropped to a penny. Then people began to send valentines. Soon, more and more people celebrated Valentine's Day.

Valentine's Day Comes to America

In the 1700s, Americans often got valentines from their friends in England. They had no time to celebrate Valentine's Day, however. They were too busy trying to survive in their new country. Valentine's Day didn't catch on in America until much later. In many of the first American valentines, men asked women to marry them.

American Valentines

Americans liked to make valentines called the "true-love knot" and the "endless-love knot." People who made these valentines drew hearts connected at the sides. They wrote words of love along the edges of the hearts.

Another American valentine was the "pinprick" valentine. A pinprick valentine was made by poking holes in the edges of paper with a sewing needle.

Others made "acrostic" valentines. The first letter of the first word on each line spelled out their sweethearts' names.

Later, valentines were made by machine. Between 1906 and 1919, American factories began making valentine cards. Companies such as Hallmark, American Greetings, and Gibson started then.

Things You Might See on Valentine's Day

Hearts

The heart is a favorite **symbol** of Valentine's Day. A long time ago, people thought our souls lived in our hearts. Some people believed that the power to think and feel came from the heart too.

Today, we still talk as if our hearts had feelings. We say a mean person is "heartless." Or we say a kind and giving person has a "big heart."

Flowers

Sweet-smelling flowers remind people of love. Over the years, the red rose has become the flower of love. It smells sweet.

Many people think red is the best color to show love. It is the color of the human heart.

Cupid

Cupid is pictured as a chubby baby boy. He has wings on his back. He carries a bow and arrow.

Cupid was a Roman god. His mother was Venus, the Roman goddess of love and beauty. Cupid's father was Mars, the Roman god of war.

Cupid was a happy little god. He wanted others to be happy too. He shot **invisible** arrows into people's hearts and made them fall in love.

Birds

Birds remind us of spring and mating. In the past, people believed that birds chose a **mate** on Saint Valentine's Day. In those days, the holiday was closer to spring. Spring is the time when birds mate and build their nests.

People liked to draw doves on their handmade valentines. Doves are a symbol of love. They sit together in pairs. Doves make gentle, cooing sounds to each other.

What You Can Do on Valentine's Day

The way we celebrate February 14 has changed since Roman times. We no longer celebrate spring on this day. It is no longer a day just for sweethearts. Valentine's Day is now a holiday for everyone.

Getting and giving candy and cards on Valentine's Day is fun. You can do many other things on Valentine's Day. Here are some ideas:

* Make your own valentine for someone special.
* Bring flowers to someone you haven't visited in a long time.
* Forgive someone who has hurt you.
* Visit a neighbor who is lonely or sick.
* Do something special to show a family member, a friend, or a teacher that you care about that person.

Glossary

celebrate to have a party or honor a special event

Christians people who believe that Jesus Christ is the son of God

customs things that members of a group usually do

emperor a ruler of an empire

festival a holiday or celebration

invisible something that cannot be seen

mate one of a pair

patron saint a holy person who helps others

shepherds people who take care of sheep

sweethearts lovable people

symbol something that stands for something else

valentine a card or gift that one gives a loved one on Valentine's Day

Where You Can Learn
More about Valentine's Day

At the Library

Bulla, Clyde Robert. *The Story of Valentine's Day*. New York: HarperCollins Publishers, 1999.

Kalman, Bobbie. *We Celebrate Valentine's Day*. New York: Crabtree Publishing Company, 1994.

Roop, Peter and Connie. *Let's Celebrate Valentine's Day*. Brookfield, Conn.: The Millbrook Press, 1999.

On the Web

HOLIDAYS ON THE WEB: *http://www.holidays.net*

For links that relate to Valentine's Day history, songs, crafts, and food

MERPY'S VALENTINE CELEBRATION: *http://www.merpy.com/valentine/*

For information about how to make your own cards for Valentine's Day

THE SUPERSITE FOR KIDS: *http://www.bonus.com/bonus/list/holiday_valentines.html*

For fun activities and games related to Valentine's Day

Index

"acrostic" valentines, 22

American customs, 22

Austrian customs, 12, 15

birds, 27

Christians, 6, 12

Cupid (Roman god), 26

customs, 12, 15, 22

doves, 27

Duke of Orleans, 17

"endless-love knot" valentines, 22

English customs, 12

flowers, 25, 29

French customs, 15

hearts, 24

Hungarian customs, 12, 15

Italian customs, 12

Lupercalia festival, 5

Mars (Roman god), 26

"pinprick" valentines, 22

saints, 7, 15

"true-love knot" valentines, 22

Valentine (saint), 6-7, 9-11

valentine writers, 17

valentines, 4, 17-18, 21-22, 29

Venus (Roman goddess), 26

About the Author and Illustrator

Alice K. Flanagan writes books for children and teachers. Since she was a young girl, she has enjoyed writing. She has written more than seventy books. Some of her books include biographies of U.S. presidents and their wives, biographies of people working in our neighborhoods, phonics books for beginning readers, and informational books about birds and Native Americans. Alice K. Flanagan lives in Chicago, Illinois.

Shelley Dieterichs has always had a special interest in illustrating for children. She has illustrated several well-known children's books. She has also launched a line of stationery products for children with her own illustrations and created special products for families built by adoption. Shelley Dieterichs lives in St. Louis, Missouri.